THE FACTS ABOUT

DEATH

BY
Gail B. Stewart

EDITED BY
Anita Larsen

CONSULTANT
Elaine Wynne, M.A., Licensed Psychologist

CRESTWOOD HOUSE
New York

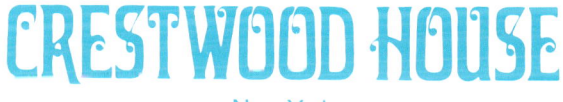

CIP
LIBRARY OF CONGRESS CATALOGING IN PUBLICATION DATA

Stewart, Gail B.
  Death

  (The facts about)
  Includes index.
  SUMMARY: Discusses death as a natural occurence, what happens when someone dies, and how to deal with feelings of fear and grief.
  1. Death — Juvenile literature. [1. Death.] I. Title. II. Series.
  HQ1073.3.S74   1989   306.9—dc19   89-31257
  ISBN 0-89686-446-4

PHOTO CREDITS

Cover: Berg & Associates: Alfred Hochrein
Third Coast Stock Source: (Todd S. Dacquisto) 4, 35;
  (Grace Natoli-Sheldon) 11; (Kent DuFault) 30; (MacDonald Photography) 33; (Jack Hamilton) 36
The Image Works: (Alan Carey) 9; (Bob Daemmrich) 12; (Eastcott/ Momatiuk) 24; (Willie Hill, Jr.) 27; (W. Marc Bernsau) 41; (Margot Granitsas) 42
Berg & Associates: (David Stone) 19
FPG International: (Kenneth Garrett) 20

Copyright © 1989 by Crestwood House, Macmillan Publishing Company

All rights reserved. No part of this book may be reproduced or transmitted in any form or by any means, electronic or mechanical, including photocopying, recording, or by any information storage and retrieval system, without permission in writing from the Publisher.

Macmillan Publishing Company
866 Third Avenue
New York, NY 10022
Collier Macmillan Canada, Inc.

Produced by Carnival Enterprises
Printed in the United States of America
First Edition
10 9 8 7 6 5 4 3 2 1

TABLE OF CONTENTS

Kim's Story 4
The Cycle of Life 9
Not Just Old People 13
Knowing for Sure 14
Reversing Death? 16
The Physical Effects 18
Immediately after a Death 21
The Funeral Director 22
Good-byes 25
Cremation 28
A Deep Sadness 29
Extending Grief 35
Fearing Death 37
Hospices 38
What Then? 39
The Importance of Life 42
For More Information 43
Glossary/Index 44-46

The subject of death is hard to talk about because it makes many people uneasy. But by asking questions about death, perhaps we can remove some of its mystery.

KIM'S STORY

"See you later, Mom!" yelled Kim as she ran out the front door. "I'm going to see Grandma."

Letting the screen door slam behind her, Kim ran out to the garage and unlocked her bike. It had been almost a week since she'd seen her grandmother. Usually on Tuesdays and Fridays Kim rode her bike to school and stopped at her grandmother's on the way home. This week, however, her grandmother had had doctors' appointments, so their get-together was postponed until this Saturday afternoon.

Kim had always enjoyed a special relationship with her grandmother. They both loved watching old movies. Grandma had a subscription to a movie magazine—her one weakness, she said, was reading about movie stars—and sometimes they paged through those magazines together. Other times they played Monopoly or watched TV.

But the best times were the evenings they spent reading. Grandma sat in her big blue and yellow overstuffed chair with her feet up. Kim lounged on the sofa, covered with an afghan. They'd make a pot of tea and cinnamon toast and just read. Often hours would go by, with neither of them saying a word. Some girls her age might have thought this was silly or dull, but not Kim. To her, Grandma was really a friend, someone Kim knew she could always talk to without being criticized or judged.

Kim easily biked the five miles to her grandmother's apartment building. In her school backpack she carried a book she'd been wanting to start for a long time, as well as a mix for gingerbread. That would taste good with the tea later on, Kim thought happily.

Once there, Kim locked her bike, then took the stairs two at a time up to the third floor. She knocked on Grandma's door. No answer. Probably Grandma was in the bathroom. Kim paced the hall a while, looking at the other doors and the pictures on the walls.

After several minutes Kim knocked again. Still no answer. Kim was confused. Grandma knew she was coming; they had talked about it on the phone just a couple of days ago. She couldn't have forgotten. And she wouldn't have gone out, because her arthritis made walking very painful. Where was she, then?

As Kim stood wondering what to do, Mrs. Hathaway, Grandma's neighbor, opened her door down the hall.

"Why, Kim," called Mrs. Hathaway, "Nice to see you. Going to visit your grandma?"

"Yes, but Mrs. Hathaway," said Kim, "do you know where she is? I've been knocking but nobody answers."

"Oh, dear," said Mrs. Hathaway. "I hope she hasn't fallen. Wait right here. I'll get the extra key."

When she returned, it seemed to take ages to open Grandma's door. When they finally did, Kim walked in, calling, "Grandma! Are you all right? I'm here." Somehow, the words sounded strange, as though she were someone else speaking.

It was Mrs. Hathaway who discovered Grandma in bed, still in her nightgown. At first it appeared as though she were still asleep, but she was too still. Her mouth was slightly open, and her eyes were shut. Even Kim, who had never seen a dead person except on television, knew right away. Grandma was dead.

The rest of the afternoon passed very quickly, almost as if it were a dream. The paramedics arrived and took Grandma's body away. They would first take her to the hospital, where it would be determined how she died. One of the paramedics told Kim that Grandma must have died in her sleep, and that she probably had felt no pain at all.

Mrs. Hathaway called Kim's parents, and they came right away. Lots of neighbors came out of their apartments to see what all the noise was about. More people were outside, curious about the reason for the ambulance.

Kim was numb. She couldn't feel anything at all. Her mother and Mrs. Hathaway cried. Strangers inside Grandma's apartment talked about her in the past tense: "She was...." At last, Kim was back home, the gingerbread mix still in her backpack.

No one in Kim's family had ever died, nor had any member of her friends' families. Kim had had a goldfish once that died, but that wasn't the same. Never had Kim felt so mixed up, so full of questions.

What had happened to Grandma? Had she suffered as she died? What would happen to her now? Would she go to heaven? Kim couldn't remember her grandmother ever mentioning heaven. What would happen to her body? Would she be buried? Who would make those decisions? How could Kim go on with her life as if nothing had happened?

The world, which had only yesterday seemed like such a friendly place, suddenly seemed frightening and cold.

* * *

The subject of death usually makes people uncomfortable. When something makes us feel uneasy, we tend not to talk about it much, or if we do, we might joke about it.

Probably the biggest reason for our unwillingness to discuss death is that it is largely a mystery. Doctors can tell us *why* a person died, but no one has been able to show what, if anything, happens after death. What does it feel like to die? Is there a life after death, as some religions believe? Not knowing the answers to these questions can make us afraid.

Another reason we avoid the subject is that it makes us sad. Someone dead is never coming back. We'll never see that person again. It makes us sad to think that our time with that person is over, and that our lives will feel empty. It's especially hard when the dead person is a member of the family—a grandparent, a parent, a brother or sister, or even our own child.

But there is a good reason to discuss death, and to ask questions about it. There are many things we do know about death. Some of the things we know might make the subject less scary. We can learn about the ways doctors know a person has died. (It's not as easy as you might think.)

We can find out about *funerals,* and about the ways a body is prepared for the funeral. We can also learn about the kinds of feelings people have when someone they love has died.

By knowing some of these things and by asking questions, we can remove some of the mystery of death. "Death is as common as life," one proverb says. When we see death as a natural part of our world, the fact of death can make a little more sense.

THE CYCLE OF LIFE

Anything or anyone that lives eventually dies. That goes for rose bushes, dogs, fish, maple trees, people—everything and everybody that is alive.

Scientists say there are four stages a living thing goes through in its life—birth, growth, aging, and death.

Death is the last step in the aging process. It happens to every living thing.

Death is the last step in the aging process that begins almost the moment we are born. Babies begin to lose skin cells and red blood cells by the millions their first day. Children grow so fast in so many different ways, however, that the aging of their bodies is almost invisible. At the age of 20, we are the strongest, the most physically fit we can be. Everything is working at its peak.

But not long after that, usually in our 30s, the telltale signs of age begin to show. Very gradually our eyes may not work as well. We may need glasses when before we didn't. Hair may become thinner, or turn gray. Our skin isn't as elastic as it once was, so wrinkles begin to appear around our mouths and eyes. Our bodies don't require as many calories as they used to, so unless we change our eating habits, we easily put on extra weight.

This aging slowly progresses from the inconvenience of wrinkles, gray hair, and glasses to more severe changes that make our bodies work less efficiently. As people get older and older, their organs don't work as well as they once did. Blood doesn't circulate as well as it used to, food doesn't digest as well, and so on. Eventually, the system breaks down, or *deteriorates,* and the person finally dies.

This may sound depressing, but it's really not. The changes come about gradually, over a long, long period of time. People talk about "old age creeping up on you," and that's exactly what they mean. Old age isn't a disease. Instead, it is a body working as long as it was designed to work! Many people live healthy lives into their 80s, 90s, and even older!

People like Kim, who have had someone close to them die, naturally wonder why anyone has to die. It seems unfair to be separated forever from those we love. Wouldn't it be great if scientists could invent a way for people to live forever? No one would ever die or have to say good-bye to loved ones.

But that wouldn't be great at all—for a couple of reasons. First, if people never died, there would soon be no space left. Their children would have children, and those children would have children, and those, and

Slowly, our bodies age and deteriorate. The change comes over a long, long period of time.

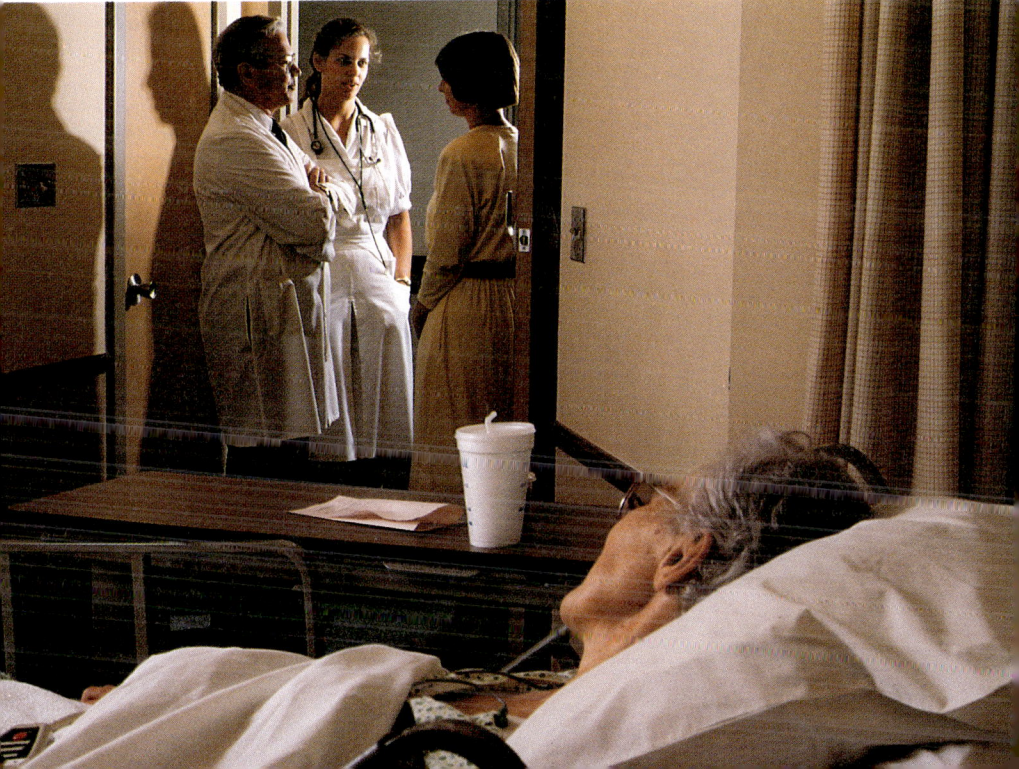

those. Cities and towns would be packed so full there would be no place for all of us to live. Where would we get the energy to heat our homes? And what would we eat? Surely there wouldn't be nearly enough farmland to grow food for this gigantic population.

Nature has built in death to make room for the young and strong. To tamper with that balance would create more problems than it could ever solve.

Death serves another function besides creating space. Among humans, at least, the notion that we are going to die gives our lives more purpose. We know we are not going to be here forever, so our lives are more important. They are limited by time.

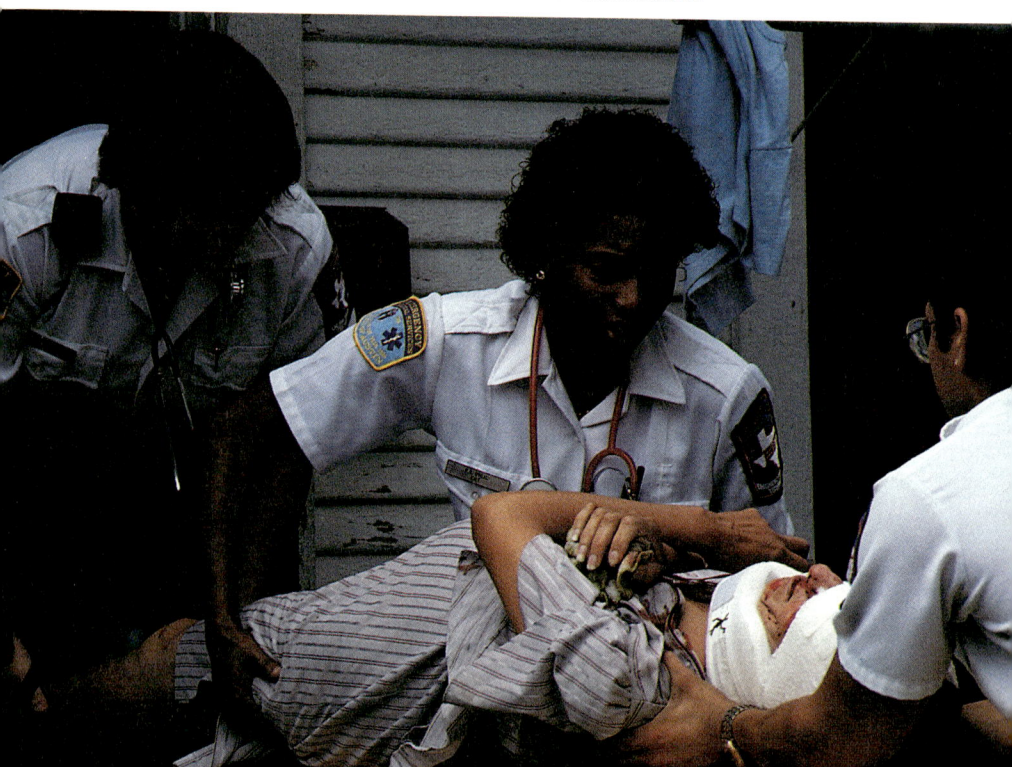

About 5,000 people in the United States die every day — some from old age and others from accidents or illnesses.

NOT JUST OLD PEOPLE

Every minute in the United States, about four people die. That works out to over 5,000 people every day. Many of these people die from the effects of old age, but young people also die. A baby dies from an infection, a two-year-old drowns in a swimming pool, a young man dies of AIDS. There are many ways of dying, and they are not all related to disease or old age.

In the United States, the three leading causes of death among adults are heart disease, cancer, and strokes. Among children, accidents cause the most deaths; cancer is the second leading cause. Our country keeps statistics that show how many people every year die of a particular cause. By looking at these statistics, we can see how our nation's health has changed over the years. We can also see how our *mortality rate,* or death rate, compares to that of other nations.

For example, contagious diseases like *influenza* (the long name for what we call "flu") used to be extremely deadly. Thousands of people, many of them small children, died in flu epidemics. But health care in much of the world, and especially in this country, has greatly improved. Scientists know more about the ways in which diseases spread. They can isolate germs to study them more carefully. Modern medicine has even created vaccines and super-drugs to fight diseases that used to be deadly. Yet for all the advances we've made in health care, medical technology, and nutrition, we still cannot eliminate death.

"There are just too many ways our bodies are vulnerable," says one doctor. "Just when we thought we could push Mother Nature back with a cure for smallpox, and another for polio, we are hit with cancer and AIDS. Maybe in the next decade we'll see cures for those diseases, I don't know. But I do know that there will always be something—some new virus lurking around that will give us fits. People have to realize that medicine is not a god. We can't work miracles. The human body doesn't come with a warranty, like a new car."

KNOWING FOR SURE

Tina was baby-sitting her little sister one afternoon, and the two girls were outside in the back yard. Four-year-old Rachel suddenly began calling for Tina. She had discovered a dead robin near the tree trunk.

"Oh, Rachel, don't pick it up."

"How come?" the little girl wanted to know. She had never been this close to a robin before, and she wanted to hold it.

"Because the poor bird is dead," Tina told her. "He probably died in the storm last night."

"No, he isn't. He's just quiet," said Rachel stubbornly.

"No, Rach—see, he doesn't move at all. He's dead."

The little girl was confused. "Maybe he's just sleeping. Maybe he'll wake up soon."

Tina shook her head. "He'll never wake up. See, he's stiff. He isn't breathing, and his heart isn't beating anymore. You may yell and poke and everything you want, but he'll never wake up. That's what being dead means."

It used to be that simple for humans, too. A doctor used to listen for a heartbeat or feel for a pulse. Sometimes a feather or a mirror was held under the person's nostrils. If the mirror got cloudy or the feather moved a bit, that was evidence that the person was still breathing.

But as medical technology has gotten more complicated, so have our definitions of death. If a person isn't breathing, we have machines that can do that for him or her. If the heart has stopped beating, we can sometimes start it again with a shot of medicine or a jolt of electricity. Then how do we really know when death has come?

To understand about death, we need to understand the basics of a living human body. Scientists know that our bodies are made of billions of cells. These cells are in our blood, our brains, our skin, our muscles—everywhere. The cells in our blood carry food and oxygen to the cells in the rest of our bodies. The heart pumps these red blood cells throughout our bodies.

When the flow of blood stops, the body's supply of oxygen and food is cut off and soon the cells will begin to die. The flow of blood may stop because of an accident—perhaps some important blood vessel has been damaged so blood cannot get through. Or the person may have suffered a heart attack, so the heart can no longer pump blood. Or a tumor may have interfered somehow with the movement of the cells.

At any rate, the stopping of the heart results in something called *clinical death,* which is the first of two stages of death. When a person is clinically dead, the heart doesn't pump, so there is no heartbeat and no pulse. Breathing stops.

REVERSING DEATH?

Many times clinical deaths do not result in permanent death, however. If a person whose breathing and heartbeat have stopped gets help quickly, death can actually be reversed.

Doctors can sometimes restart a stopped heart with medicine. Sometimes they use a machine that sends an electrical current through the heart, and it starts that way. Heart massage, too, can be successful in reviving the heart.

Breathing can be started again also. Sometimes doctors make a small opening in the person's throat and insert a plastic tube. The tube is hooked up to a *respirator,* which is a machine that can "breathe" for a person until the person is able to breathe without it. Respirators and other equipment that keep a person's heart and breathing going are called *life support*.

Doctors know that life-support systems are important and useful as long as the person's brain has not died. If several minutes have gone by without the brain receiving any oxygen, however, brain cells rapidly begin to die.

The brain, as you probably know, is the control center for your body. Our abilities to learn, to think, to recognize our friends and families, to remember, even to breathe are all centered in the brain. In a healthy person's brain, there are small electric charges called *brain waves* going on all the time. If someone has been in an accident or has been injured in some way, the brain might die. In other words, the brain would no longer be creating those brain waves.

Scientists have developed a machine that can measure how much activity is going on in a person's brain. The machine, called an *electroencephalograph (EEG,* for short), is connected by wires to the outside of a person's scalp. If the brain is sending out any of those little electric charges, they will be recorded on a graph in the EEG. The graph of a healthy brain looks like a squiggly line, with lots of ups and downs. If the brain is not alive, however, the graph will look like a straight line. In such a case, the person is said to be *brain dead.*

Brain death is considered the final stage of death. Unlike clinical death, brain death cannot be reversed. Brain cells cannot repair themselves, nor can the brain grow new cells to replace dead ones. A person who is clinically dead, but whose brain still shows activity on an EEG, can be hooked up to life-support systems in the hope that he or she can get well. A person whose brain showed no EEG activity could be "kept alive" by those same machines. However, there would be no hope that he or she would ever really be alive again. Certainly, the heart may pump, and the respirator might force air in and out of the lungs, but it would be only mechanical.

In cases like this, hospital officials and the families of the patient usually agree that the life-support systems should be turned off. No one, they say, is served by forcing life into a body that is dead.

THE PHYSICAL EFFECTS

When a person is dead, the body gradually changes. Like all living things, a human body is made up of material that will eventually *decompose,* or decay. You may have seen how grass cuttings and dead plants in the yard decay until they are part of the soil. This is very much like what happens to the body of a dead animal or person.

Before the body decays, however, there are noticeable changes. For one thing, the skin appears very pale. This is because the blood is not being circulated through the body any longer. The blood collects under the skin in

We may remember a person who has died by visiting his or her grave.

blotchy areas. This is especially true with the fingertips, the nose, and toes. They all take on sort of a bluish tint from the lack of blood flowing in them.

The dead body is no longer warm to the touch. It gradually becomes the same temperature as the air around it.

If you've ever seen or touched a dead animal, you know that they get very stiff and hard. This happens with people, too, after they've been dead a couple of hours. The skin isn't really hard, it's just a reflex of all of the muscles stiffening. This is called *rigor mortis,*

19

After a death, the family arranges for the dead person's funeral and burial.

which is Latin for "the stiffness of death." Rigor mortis goes away after about a day.

All of these physical effects are strange to us, and maybe they make us a bit afraid. It's important to remember that a body's decomposing and decay are as much a part of the cycle of life as is birth.

In her book *The Tenth Good Thing About Barney,* Judith Viorst tells about a child whose cat has died. The child decides that it would help make him less sad by remembering ten good things about the cat. It takes him awhile, but he comes up with nine good things—

ranging from the friendship and love Barney provided to the silly tricks he'd do.

Yet it wasn't until Barney had been buried in the yard that the little boy was able to identify the tenth good thing about his cat. Plainly speaking, it was that in death, because of his gradual decomposition, Barney would be helping their flowers grow.

IMMEDIATELY AFTER A DEATH

Whenever anyone in this country dies, authorities must fill out a piece of paper called a *death certificate*. The death certificate lists the person's name and address, as well as the time and place of the death. Death certificates are kept on file by the government, just like birth certificates and marriage certificates.

If the person has died in a hospital, the doctor fills it out. If the person died and the cause is not known right away, the authorities might request an *autopsy*. An autopsy is a kind of examination done only on dead bodies. In an autopsy, doctors cut open the body and study it carefully. They may remove many of the organs and study some of the cells under a microscope. In this way, they can be certain of the exact cause of the person's death. After the autopsy, the organs are put back, and the body is sewn up.

Autopsies are often helpful in cases where police suspect murder. If a person died from drugs, an autopsy can tell that, too. Sometimes, if the death was unexpected, a family might request the hospital to perform an autopsy. The results might answer questions about their loved one's death.

THE FUNERAL DIRECTOR

Once known as a mortician or an undertaker, the *funeral director* is the person who prepares the body for burial. After the death certificate is signed and any needed autopsy is performed, the funeral director takes the body to a place called a *funeral home*. There the body will be *embalmed*. Embalming is the process of removing the blood and replacing it with chemicals that will slow down the body's decay.

Embalming is an ancient custom, dating back at least 6,000 years before Christ. The Egyptians believed that if the body were not preserved, the soul would also die. For that reason, they perfected a system of embalming resulting in *mummies*. The mummy was a body that had been preserved with various chemicals, then wrapped in fine cloth. The entire process of embalming for the ancient Egyptians took 70 days.

Today, we don't believe it's important to preserve the body for another life. Once the body is dead, it must be disposed of. Most of the time, the family and friends of the person who has died wish to have a special service, called a funeral, to remember and honor the dead person.

The family usually meets with the funeral director to discuss the plans for the funeral. They decide on the type of *casket* in which to bury the body. A casket is really nothing more than a long box. Some are fancy, made of expensive wood with satin or silk pillows inside and shiny gold handles outside. Other caskets are plainer, made of a thin layer of metal or pine.

The funeral director must help the family make sensible decisions at a sad time for them. He must help them arrange for the public announcement of the death in the newspaper, called an *obituary*. He must ask the family to choose clothing in which to bury the body. He and the family must discuss whether or not to have the casket open during the funeral. He must see to it that everything related to the funeral of this person goes smoothly and easily.

"I see my job as very important," says Paul Mallory, a funeral director from Chicago. "If I've done my job right, if I've paid attention to all the details, I've helped the family in their time of sorrow. I'm a strong believer in sharing the experience of sadness at a time of death. My preparing the body for the last time friends and family will see it is a big responsibility."

GOOD-BYES

Lisa was 13 when her father died in a car crash. She was staying overnight at a friend's house the night it happened. When her mother came over late that night to tell her, Lisa couldn't believe it.

"I kept thinking, this is wrong. My dad's in great shape. He was a runner—he'd run five miles every morning. My mom must be wrong. The policeman who came to tell my mother must have been wrong.

"It took awhile for it to sink in. I think the best thing that happened was the funeral. I know that sounds weird, but it helped me."

Lisa had been sure that seeing her father in a casket in a church would be frightening. She wanted to remember him as alive and strong. At first she told her mother she didn't want to go to the funeral. Her mother respected her feelings, but told her that by being there, Lisa would be helping the whole family.

"It was helpful for me to see all our friends, all the people he worked with. My principal came, and so did lots of the kids in my class. I felt a little less mixed up."

Funerals can be fancy and elaborate or small and personal. Most funerals take place in a funeral home or a house of worship, but some families prefer to hold the service in their homes. Sometimes the casket is open, allowing the family and friends to see the person one last time. If, however, the person has died after a long illness or because of a violent accident, he or she

At a funeral, people gather to honor the dead person.

might look different. In cases like these, the family usually decides to have the casket closed at the funeral.

There is usually a time for music and maybe a prayer. Often the family tries to include readings and music that the person enjoyed during life.

"My uncle was a jazz piano player," said 15-year-old Neal. "When he died, we knew that sad violin music or organ preludes wouldn't fit him at all. We chose lots of loud, happy songs by Fats Waller and other famous pianists. I felt kind of important, because my aunt let me help choose the ones I thought he would have liked. The funeral was a little sad—I think everyone there missed my uncle a lot. But mostly it was kind of uplifting. I liked saying good-bye to my uncle like that."

After the funeral service, the casket is taken by a special car, called a *hearse,* to the cemetery. Since the casket is quite heavy, several people carry it, using the handles on the sides. Usually the family asks friends of the person who died to be the casket carriers, called *pallbearers.* To be asked to be a pallbearer is considered an honor.

The pallbearers carry the casket to the hearse, and then people proceed to the cemetery. Often, the cemetery is some distance from the funeral home or house of worship, so people get in their cars and drive, following the hearse, which is the lead car. Some states require that the funeral parade, or *cortege,* keep their car lights on so other drivers will not break through the procession by mistake.

Pallbearers are usually friends or relatives of the dead person. They carry the casket from the hearse to the grave site.

At the cemetery, the pallbearers remove the casket from the hearse and carry it to the grave site. Sometimes a few more prayers or readings are said. Sometimes people will stand silently for a few minutes. This is an act of respect, to honor the person who has died by thinking about him or her.

Sometimes, a handful of dirt or sand is thrown on the casket, as well as flowers. Sometimes another song will be played or sung. Each of these customs is meant to show that people are saying good-bye to someone whom they loved. By doing it together, they try to lend one another support.

CREMATION

Not all people choose to be buried when they die. Many people think that with shortages of land and space in many of our cities, it's more sensible not to waste space burying people in cemeteries. Instead, they choose *cremation,* which is the destruction of the dead body by fire.

It's certainly not a new way to dispose of a body. Ancient Greeks and Romans cremated their dead, as did many ancient tribes in Africa. People in ancient India cremated their dead and scattered the ashes on the Ganges River, which they believed to be sacred. The Vikings long ago put dead warriors on boats and set them afire before pushing them out to sea.

Cremation fires were even the source of another custom in India, called *suttee.* This practice encouraged the wife of a dead man to throw herself on the fire. It was believed that by killing herself, she could make up for all her husband's past sins. By committing *suttee,* she could help him get to paradise. That custom was outlawed by the government in India many years ago, but people from India say it is still practiced today in some villages.

Today in the United States, about 8 percent of all

people who die are cremated. This contrasts sharply with Japan, where over 85 percent are cremated, and England, where the number is about 70 percent.

Bodies are cremated in special furnaces, which burn at extremely hot temperatures—about 2,500 degrees F. The furnace, or crematorium, is made of brick. There are tubes carrying gas inside the furnace. If a body is to be cremated, a wood casket is used. The body in its casket is placed in the furnace, and the doors are sealed.

In about two hours, the body is reduced to ashes and tiny pieces of bone fragments. Sometimes these ashes are buried inside a box in a special grave. Other times the ashes are kept in an urn, or vase, by the family. Often, the family decides to scatter the ashes in a place that was special to their loved one. Members of one family scattered their grandmother's ashes in a wildlife sanctuary that the woman had always loved.

A DEEP SADNESS

When someone you know has died, especially someone you know well, you may have many different feelings. On television or in the movies, people cry when they are told about the death of someone they cared about. After the characters cry, they usually say they feel a whole lot better. They act stronger, better able to go on with their lives.

Grief is the deep sadness we feel when someone we know has died.

Scenes like these are different from the way most people act when someone close to them has died. In fact, there are many, many different ways that people can act when they feel this sadness, called *grief*. Some people may be withdrawn and quiet, while others are loud and aggressive. Some people get physically ill, suffering from upset stomachs and headaches.

What makes grief different from any other sadness?

"When my little sister died, I didn't tell anyone how bad I felt," remembers 11-year-old Jason. "I just stayed out of everybody's way. When I was by myself, I just sat on my bed and stared out the window. It was the biggest, saddest feeling. It was like deep sadness and pain all rolled into one. The only thing I can say is that after awhile it goes away. I still hurt, but not all the time."

Sometimes other people expect us to grieve in a way they can understand. If we don't show our emotions in the same way they do, we might wonder about our own feelings. When Michelle's grandfather died, her family was very open about their grief. Her mother and father both cried at the funeral. Many of her grandfather's friends were there, and they had tears in their eyes, too. But Michelle didn't cry.

"My cousin asked me, 'How come you just stood there? You didn't even cry at all. You must not have loved Grandpa as much as I did.' That made me mad," said Michelle. "I loved Grandpa a lot, or at least I thought I did. When my cousin said that, it made me wonder if there was something wrong with me. I still felt sad inside, but there weren't any tears."

Sometimes our grief at losing someone we loved is mixed up with other emotions. For instance, we may feel angry at the person for leaving us alone. It may make no sense to talk about it. How can we be angry at someone who is dead, who did us no harm? But the feelings are still there. It makes us feel as if we were abandoned.

Paul was ten when his mother died. The family knew she was dying. She had been sick with cancer for more than a year. Her death wasn't a shock to anyone. But Paul began acting differently than he had before when his mother was sick. He picked fights with his older brother and was rude to his teachers in school.

"My dad finally made me sit down and tell him what it was that was making me act so bad," said Paul. "He said, 'Are you mad at somebody? Did somebody do something wrong?' I told him it made me mad that Mom had died. I hated it that I had to be home every morning for 20 minutes all by myself. My dad leaves for work, and then my brother takes the early bus. I hated the house being empty, and I hated not seeing my mom ever. Every time one of my friends mentioned his mom it made me mad at mine for dying."

When we are sad because our feelings are hurt, or because we are embarrassed in front of our friends, that feeling comes all at once. Grief is different, because we may not feel the sadness until much later—long after the person we love has died.

Emily Brown's husband died after a heart attack. He was 75 when he died. Although Emily and her husband were close, she didn't show sadness at all in the days following his death. She arranged for the funeral and called her children and her friends to let them know what had happened. She bustled about the house, cleaning and baking in preparation for the visitors that would be coming.

"I was in a trance, I think," says Emily. "I didn't feel anything. It was as if I were numb or something. Peo-

Sometimes, people do not show their grief right away. They may finally face their deep sadness much later.

ple would talk about Arthur's death, and I knew I should be feeling something, but I just didn't. I thought, well, this isn't going to be so bad after all.

"You know when his death hit me? Opening Day for the White Sox! I cried like a baby. It was then—almost two months after Arthur died—that it dawned on me I'd never see him again. We always used to listen to the games on the radio, and I guess I thought, well, Arthur's not here, and he'll never be here."

Some psychologists think our brains protect us from shock and grief by screening them out until we can cope with them. Children, especially very young children, appear not to feel much sadness or grief when they are told someone has died.

Pete's father was a policeman. He was killed while chasing a burglary suspect one night. When his mother came into his room to tell him what had happened, Pete's reaction surprised them both.

"Mom said Dad had been shot, and that he was dead. I said, in a very quiet voice, that I hoped she wasn't going to get married ever again, because I didn't want a new dad, and I didn't want to move! I didn't say anything about Dad. I didn't even ask how it happened till about a year later. I just wanted to make sure my life wasn't going to change too much."

Pete remembers feeling more proud than sad at his father's funeral. "I liked walking into the church for the funeral. I knew everybody was looking at our family, and I felt kind of important. It was the same at school. Kids would say, 'There's the kid whose father got shot.' I felt a little bit like a hero.

"But that didn't last long. The sadness came in waves, like in the ocean. I'd be standing up at the board in math class doing a problem, and all of a sudden I'd have this feeling like my chest was caving in. I wanted to cry and yell and throw things. I needed to get out of there fast! My teachers were really nice, and they understood how I felt. That part of the sadness has gone away. I miss my dad a lot, but I don't ache all the time anymore."

EXTENDING GRIEF

Doctors and *psychologists* who know a great deal about grieving say there is no best way to be sad or to miss the person who has died. If tears help, then cry. If it helps to keep busy, then do that.

One thing everybody seems to agree on is that it's not good to pretend we don't feel sad.

"Grieving is a natural response to tragedy and sorrow," said one doctor who works with cancer patients and their families. "If we keep things bottled up inside, or if we tell ourselves to 'be brave' and not cry, we'll just be extending our pain. It helps to talk to other people, or to allow ourselves to miss the person who has died. The last thing we should ever do is to act as though it never happened."

It is okay to miss the person who has died. Sometimes it helps to talk about your grief with someone else.

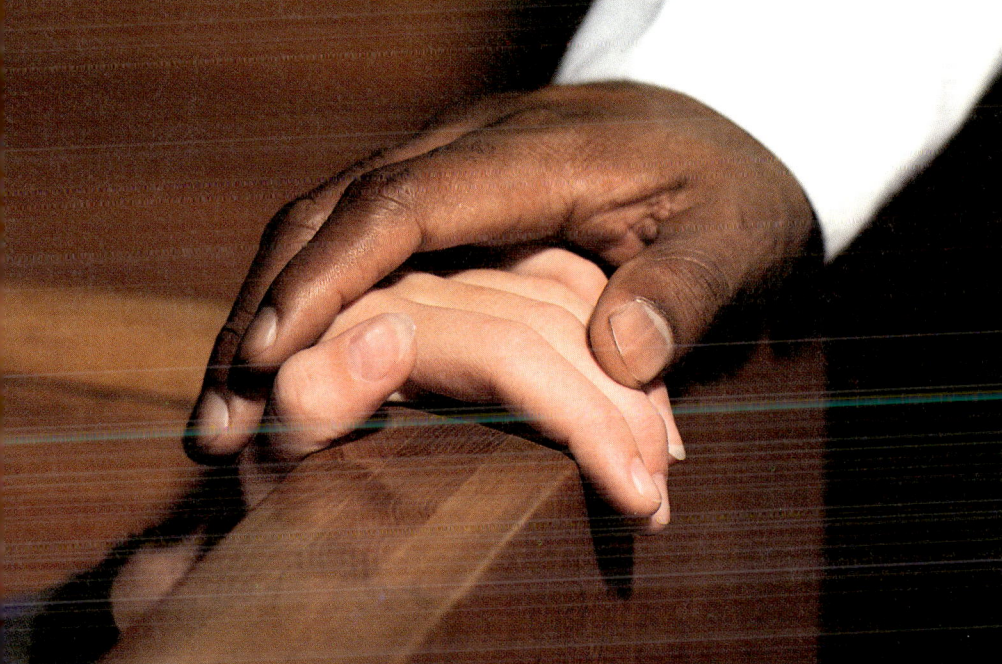

FEARING DEATH

When Gina's little brother died, her reaction was sadness mixed with fear.

"Timmy had leukemia, which is cancer of the blood," Gina says. "I used to visit him all the time in the hospital. On his good days, he was happy and excited—always talking about when he could come home. But when he was feeling sick, it was awful. He'd throw up, and he'd just lie there in his bed looking thin.

"Toward the end, the doctors told us they figured he'd die any day. There was nothing they could do. He had tubes hooked into his nose, and he was gagging all the time. I wasn't there when he died, but my mom was. I don't ever want to be sick like Timmy. I don't want to die."

Because death is such a mystery, we tend to fear it. What's more, most deaths today occur in nursing homes and hospitals. It's frightening to think of feeling sick in a place away from home. We are afraid of being alone, of being separated from our families, and of the pain and suffering that sometimes go along with dying.

In past times, people didn't go to nursing homes when they were old and sick. Hospitals were less common. Certainly, there were no amazing life-support systems to keep people alive when their lungs and hearts were weak.

In those times, people usually died at home. Grandparents lived with their children and grandchildren, or

We tend to fear death because it is such a mystery.

at least near by. When a grandma was nearing death, she was usually at home. Her family was there, talking with her, comforting her, saying good-bye to her. Being with the people who loved her must have made death a little less scary for the grandma and the family. Death wasn't such a terrifying prospect. It was natural, and it was familiar. Is that kind of death possible today?

HOSPICES

One way to make death less impersonal and less frightening is the *hospice*. A hospice is a special place for people who are going to die. The word *hospice* comes from a word used in the Middle Ages that meant "a shelter for the traveler."

The hospice is a treatment center that gives comfort to the dying and their families. Unlike a hospital, where the emphasis is on curing, or trying to cure, every patient, a hospice is for patients who can't be cured.

"In the hospital they kept wanting my grandmother to go through *chemotherapy*. That's taking lots of strong drugs to kill the cancer cells," explained 15-year-old Mary Ann. "The problem with chemotherapy is that it kills all the healthy cells, too. My grandmother was sick after her chemo treatments.

"She took herself out of the hospital and went to a hospice. She said, 'Look, I know I'm going to die. I just want to go with a little dignity.'"

Mary Ann's grandmother, like other hospice residents, was not given chemotherapy at her hospice. The atmosphere was more like a big bedroom at home than a hospital. She was encouraged to do things she liked to do, like playing the piano and visiting with her friends.

As she got closer to death, and her pain increased, Mary Ann's grandmother was given drugs to ease her suffering. In hospitals, drugs that can relieve pain are given very sparingly. Doctors worry that patients might become addicted to them. As a result, many patients suffer.

At the hospice, addiction is not a problem, since the residents are dying. Counselors and staff volunteers are always nearby to talk to a resident or family members.

"The doctor and counselor from the hospice came to my grandmother's funeral," said Mary Ann. "They were really concerned about Grandma and about all of us. To be truthful, when I first heard about the hospice, I thought it would be a terribly depressing place, like a nursing home. But it wasn't at all. I liked going there to visit Grandma. I'm glad that since she had to die, she died in a place like that where everyone liked her and cared about her."

WHAT THEN?

Some people think of death as a beginning to a new life. In fact, most religions throughout the world believe in some afterlife, although each thinks of it in a different way.

Christians believe that when they die they will be judged on the kind of life they lead on earth. The souls, or spirits, of those who lived good lives go to a place called heaven. Heaven, Christians believe, is a place where people can live forever with God. Some people believe that those who were wicked spend eternity in a fiery place called hell. There they will be punished for their evil lives. Most of what Christians believe about heaven and hell is written in Revelations, one of the books of the Bible.

In the Buddhist religion, it is believed that the soul of a dead person is reborn in another body. This is called *reincarnation.* A person can go on and on being reborn until he or she learns to live the perfect life. When this has been achieved, the spirit enters a kind of heavenly state, called *Nirvana.*

Many people admit they're not sure what to believe. The idea of an afterlife is interesting, but no one can say for sure whether one exists or not, or if it does, what it will be like. Those who have strong feelings about an afterlife say they find great comfort in their beliefs.

Statues of soldiers help us honor and remember people who have died for our country.

THE IMPORTANCE OF LIFE

The comedian W. C. Fields joked, "This world's a hard place. A fellow's lucky to get out of it alive!"

Whether you believe in an afterlife or not, it's important to think about how valuable your life is. Knowing we will all die someday can make us appreciate the time we are alive.

Fearing death and worrying about it can only make us timid about how we live our lives. Seeing death as a necessary, natural end to life can help us put things in perspective. The way we think about death often shows in the way we live!

Death is a natural end to life. If we think about it that way, it becomes less scary. We learn to accept death as part of our lives.

FOR MORE INFORMATION

For more information about death, write to:

Center for Death Education and Research
University of Minnesota
1167 Social Science Building
Minneapolis, MN 55455

GLOSSARY/INDEX

AUTOPSY 21, 22—*An examination done only on a dead body. Doctors study the organs and cells to determine the exact cause of the person's death.*

BRAIN DEATH 17—*The final stage of death, in which there is no longer any brain activity.*

BRAIN WAVES 17—*The tiny electrical impulses a healthy brain sends out.*

CASKET 23, 25, 26, 27, 29—*A long box made of wood or metal in which dead bodies are buried.*

CHEMOTHERAPY 38, 39—*A treatment for cancer patients in which powerful drugs are used to kill cancer cells.*

CLINICAL DEATH 16, 17, 18—*The absence of heartbeat and breathing.*

CORTEGE 26—*A funeral parade or procession of family and friends on their way to a cemetary.*

CREMATION 28, 29—*Disposing of a dead body by burning it.*

DEATH CERTIFICATE 21, 22—*A document stating the time, place, and cause of a person's death.*

DECOMPOSE 18, 20 — *To decay.*

DETERIORATE 10, 11 — *To worsen or decline in quality.*

ELECTROENCEPHALOGRAPH (EEG) 17, 18 — *A machine that monitors brain waves.*

EMBALMING 22—*Preserving a dead body by injecting it with certain chemicals.*

GLOSSARY/INDEX

FUNERAL 8, 20, 23, 25, 26, 31, 32, 34, 39 — *A service in which family and friends gather to remember and honor a dead person.*

FUNERAL DIRECTOR 22, 23—*A person whose job it is to prepare a body for burial.*

FUNERAL HOME 22, 25, 26—*The building where the dead body is taken. At the funeral home, the body is prepared for the funeral and for burial.*

GRIEF 30, 31, 32, 33, 34, 35 — *Emotional pain and sadness.*

HEARSE 26, 27—*A long car used in funerals to carry the casket.*

HOSPICE 38, 39—*A treatment center for dying people.*

INFLUENZA 13—*The official word for* flu.

LIFE SUPPORT 17, 18, 37—*Machines that can take over the jobs of the lungs and heart for a critically ill person.*

MORTALITY RATE 13—*Statistics kept by the government on the number of people dying and the causes of their deaths.*

MUMMIES 22—*A carefully embalmed body from ancient Egypt.*

NIRVANA 40—*A belief held by Buddhists in which a spirit is in a heavenly state.*

OBITUARY 23—*A public announcement of death in a newspaper.*

GLOSSARY/INDEX

PALLBEARER 26, 27—*One who helps carry the casket to the grave.*
PSYCHOLOGIST 35—*A person who studies human behavior.*
REINCARNATION 40—*The belief that after death a soul will be reborn in a different body.*
RESPIRATOR 16, 18—*A machine that can breathe for a person whose lungs aren't working.*
RIGOR MORTIS 19, 20—*The stiffening of the muscles after death.*
SUTTEE 28—*The practice of some Hindu women of throwing themselves on their dead husbands' cremation fires.*